KU-419-085

A Sense of Science

Exploring Light

Claire Llewellyn

W
FRANKLIN WATTS
LONDON • SYDNEY

This edition 2011 published by
Franklin Watts
338 Euston Road
London NW1 3BH

Franklin Watts Australia
Hachette Children's Books
Level 17/207 Kent Street
Sydney NSW 2000

Copyright text
© 2007 Claire Llewellyn
Copyright, design and concept
© 2007 Franklin Watts

Editor: Jeremy Smith
Art Director: Jonathan Hair
Design: Matthew Lilly
Cover and design concept:
Jonathan Hair
Photography: Ray Moller
unless otherwise stated.

Photograph credits:
Alamy: 10b, 25t,
Corbis: 6, 11t, 13b, 17b.

We would like to thank
Scallywags for their help
with the models in this book.

KINGSTON UPON THAMES
Libraries

1028259 9	
J535	PETERS
28-Nov-2011	£7.99
NM	

A CIP catalogue record
for this book is available
from the British Library.

Dewey classification: 535

ISBN: 978 1 4451 0631 1

Printed in China

Franklin Watts is a division of
Hachette Childfren's Books,
an Hachette UK company.
www.hachette.co.uk

KT 1028259 9

Contents

A light in the sky

In the morning
the Sun rises.
It gives us light.

Sunlight lets us see the world.

Warning!
Never look at the Sun. It can hurt your eyes.

Clouds can cover the sun.

Under a cloud
What changes do you see and feel when the Sun goes behind a cloud?

Light in our home

At night, the sky gets dark. Electric lamps help us to see.

A torch is a little electric lamp.

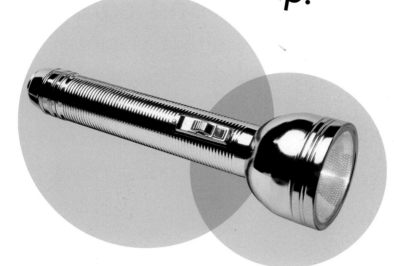

Torch play
Hide under a blanket with a torch. How do you switch it on and off? What happens when you do?

We need light in all sorts of places!

Light and heat

Most things that give out light also give out heat.

Warning!
We need to take care with hot things.

Hot and cold

Take an ice cream out of the freezer and taste it. Then leave it in the Sun for five minutes and taste again. What is different?

In summer, the Sun is very hot. Staying in the shade protects our skin.

Sun cream can also help to stop our skin burning.

We see with light

We need light to see
the world around us.
Our eyes
cannot see
in the
dark.

Can you see?
What can you see out of the kitchen
window in the daytime? What can you see
when it is dark?

We make a room darker by blocking out light.

Without natural light we need help to see things clearly.

Our eyes

We have two eyes on our face.
Our eyes have different parts.

Eyelid

Eyelashes

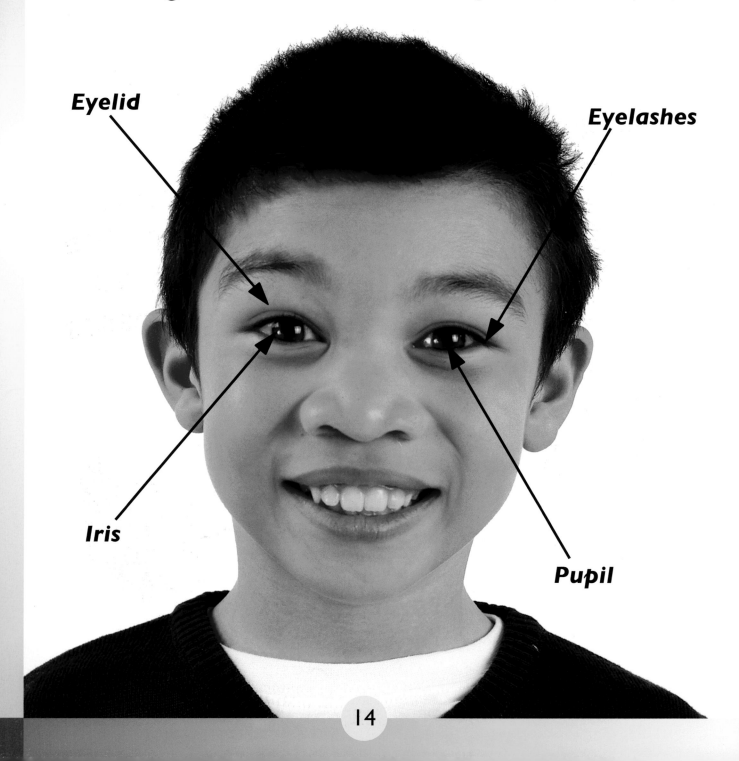

Iris

Pupil

Eye watch

Keep your eyes open but cover them with your hands. Then uncover them. What happens?

Bright light can hurt our eyes.

A cap protects our eyes from the Sun. So do sunglasses.

Feeling our way

It's hard to get around in the dark. It helps if we can feel with our hands.

Our fingers help to tell us where we are.

Touchy feely

Shut your eyes. Ask a friend to pass you some things. Can you feel what they are?

This person cannot see. He is feeling his way with a stick.

Animals at night

Many animals hunt in the dark.

An owl's big eyes help it to see at night.

Listen up!

Close your eyes. Ask a friend to move somewhere in the room and then make a tiny sound. Can you point to where they are?

A fox finds its prey at night using its nose and ears.

A bat's sharp ears help it to catch insects.

Shadows

If we stand outside on a sunny day, our body makes a shadow on the ground.

Shadows are made when something blocks the Sun's rays.

In the shade

On a sunny day, stand in the shadow of a tree. Does it feel any different from standing in the Sun?

When the Sun is low in the sky, shadows are at their longest.

An electric light makes shadows, too.

Shadows change

When we move, our shadow moves too.

It changes in all sorts of ways.

Shadow play

Make an animal shadow with your hands. Now make your animal move.

When the puppet is near an electric light, its shadow is big.

When it is farther away, its shadow is much smaller.

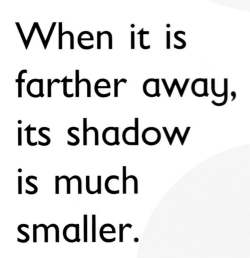

smooth and shiny

Some things are smooth and shiny.

Light makes them stand out brightly.

Mirror, mirror

Touch a mirror. What does it feel like? What happens when you shine a torch on it?

The mirror sparkles in the candlelight.

But the teddy bear does not sparkle. Its fur is rough, not smooth.

Light and life

Plants need light
to grow and survive.

Without light

With light

They do not grow properly in the dark.

Cover up

Cover a leaf on a pot plant with a piece of foil. After a week remove the foil. What can you see?

Without plants, there would be nothing for this rabbit to eat.

Without plants, and the animals that eat them, there would be nothing for us to eat either!

Glossary

Cloud

A mass of tiny water drops floating in the sky.

Electric

Worked by electricity.

Electricity

A kind of power that gives us light.

Iris

The coloured part of the eye.

Lamp

A machine that gives out light.

Pupil

A hole in the eye that lets light pass through. It looks like a black dot.

Shadow

The shape made when something blocks out light.

Shade A place where the Sun cannot reach.

Sun

The hot, bright star close to the Earth.

Torch

A small light that we can carry around.

Make a black box

1. Find an empty box and line it with black paper.

2. Make a tiny peephole in one end of the box.

3. Make a larger hole in the lid and cover it with cardboard.

4. Put a few things inside the box.

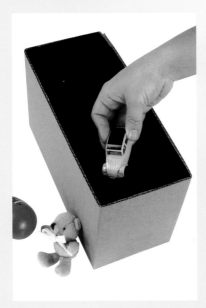

5. Ask a friend to look through the peephole. What can they see in the box?

6. Let in a little more light by moving the cardboard cover. What can be seen through the peephole now?

Index